# AUTISM IN BLACK MATTER

## FELIX NEALS

i

Cover Design by JACOB VU.

## TRIBUTES

To the many: Families who underwrote my life: Neals, Wilson, Harris, Johnson, Martin, Kincade, Nelson, Leong; people who shepherded me through mazes of knowledge in the institutions – Stanton School, US Army, Idaho State University, Washburn University School of Law, Menninger Foundation, New York State government. I am very grateful.

Thank you.

Felix.

fneals@gmail.com

**THE AUTHOR.**

Felix Neals, a retired New York State civil servant, worked in several jobs: Attorney, Office of Economic Opportunity; administrative law judge; supervising administrative law judge and special deputy secretary of state, Department of State. Before government service, Felix worked for ITT (attorney and administrator of education) and RCA (administrator early-education computer applications), a joint venture with Dr. Patrick Suppes of Stanford University's Institute for Mathematical Research in the Social Sciences.

Born in Jacksonville and reared in both Jacksonville and Miami, Florida, Felix was thought to be "mentally slow" by the public during his childhood; the family explained him as "touched" and "different." In the racially segregated communities in which he lived, there were few educational and medical resources. His childhood was deriding, his early education derisive, and his mental health care indigenous.

Felix enlisted in military service at an underage. He served in racially segregated, US Army units, faced summary court-martial and demotion in rank from sergeant to corporal. After a honorable discharge (WW II veteran, Pacific Theater), he earned a B.S. from Idaho State University, won a U.S. National Intercollegiate Oratory Championship, was selected to Who's Who Among Students in American Universities and Colleges, was awarded the Degree of Special Distinction in Pi Kappa Delta Honor Society, and was chosen a finalist in an annual competition of Yale University Series of Younger Poets. Felix acquired a J.D. from Washburn

University School of Law, Topeka, Kansas. It was in Topeka at the Menninger Foundation that Felix first heard the word, "autism," used instead of the terms "mental retardation" and "schizophrenia" in psychiatric evaluations. Felix describes the era in his life before "autism" as "knowledge delayed, treatment unknown, behavior ordained."

Felix's memberships included state and national administrative law judge associations. His writings include: Articles on *Psychosystematics:* (Felix's method of forging conceptual mental networks to subjugate his autism to his life); a law book, *New York Administrative Law, Executive Agencies, and the Administrative Law Judiciary*; a book of essays, short stories, and poetry, *Autistic Reflections in a Steel Mirror Reflected.*

# CONTENTS

**Papa.**


Saturday in May began for me as most days began: I awakened happily in my realm, a black demesne on West Fifth Street, a part of and apart from Jacksonville, Florida. I welcomed the day as a new day to celebrate all day.

I enjoyed being thirteen years old, living in Jacksonville on West Fifth Street with Papa and Mama, my paternal grandparents. I lived in their three-bedroom cottage home in "my room," the rear room in the house, the room in which a teenage couple, Dad (at 19) and Mother (at 17) lived just after marriage, the room in which a midwife delivered their only child – Me! That room was my room.

*My room. It was the room in which I consciously met Papa who introduced me to human relationships, to need, to pain, to weeping, to loneliness, to helplessness. Mother and Dad went out for an evening, leaving me to the care of Mama. Mama, Papa, and Great-Grandmother Brown (Mama's mother) were sitting on the front porch in their rocking chairs during the early evening of that night. I was in the crib in my room when I needed the warmth, the smell, and the milk of my mother, and I begin to cry (as usual) to let her know. She did not appear; I continued to cry. She still did not appear. No one appeared. I became fearful and began to weep. Papa grew impatient with my crying. He came into the room, picked me up from the crib, spanked me, placed me back into the crib, and left the room. My outcry arose in need, soared in fear, inflated in helplessness, intensified in pain, and extended in loneliness. That night in my room was the only time a family member struck me, was the only time I cried for anything,*

*and was the first time my spirit died and was reborn.*

My parents divorced when I was three years old. Dad, a member of a motorcycle club that promoted Black Nationalism, was a disciple of Garveyism (Marcus Garvey, Black Nationalism activist). As a Garveyite, Dad insisted that I learn to speak Swahili to prepare for our trip home, the return to Africa with the African diaspora. Mother, a Roman Catholic (so was Marcus Garvey), insisted that I learn to read Latin since she and I would not be taking an ocean voyage on Mr. Garvey's Black Star Line to return with the African diaspora to ancestral land in Africa.

Dad remarried and moved two blocks away from his parents' home in Jacksonville. Mother took me and moved to her father's home in Brown Sub, a remote Black community sixteen miles northwest beyond the city limits of Miami. I lived in Brown Sub with Mother in the home of my maternal grandfather, the Reverend Joseph Wilson, until Dad kidnapped me from a grammar school class when I was ten years old.

Dad bought a 1931, second-hand, Model A Ford car; secretively, he decided to test-drive it the 366 miles from Jacksonville to Brown Sub. He arrived in Brown Sub without anyone knowing. On the pretext of an emergency involving Mother, Dad abducted me from school, put me in his car, and began to drive back to Jacksonville. On the way, Dad stopped, called his sister,

Julius, in Jacksonville, and asked her to call my mother (Lylia) and tell her that he was taking me to Jacksonville to live with him.

Each year for the next six years, I lived with my paternal grandparents in Jacksonville nine months of a year, September through May, where I attended public, segregated schools. I lived with Mother in Brown Sub for the other three months of a year, June, July, and August. My divided living arrangement resulted from a legal agreement made to keep Dad from being charged with the criminal offense of kidnapping. That was my first involvement with the "buckra" (the law).

*After the public uproar following the Lindbergh kidnapping on May 1, 1932, state and federal governments enacted statutes (including Florida) covering kidnapping as a felony crime. Prison sentences and fines were substantial. There were some exceptions in laws for parents who abduct their minor child.*

Saturday 6:30 in the morning at 1545 West Fifth Street, everybody was up and about. Mama built a fire in the kitchen wood stove to cook the traditional breakfast that she cooked each morning of every day, grits with butter and eggs or grits with butter and fish-roe or both. Mama respected my choice of not eating eggs.

Papa, a carpenter, was fixing things (as every weekend) – the house, the fences, the chicken coup – or tending to the three, rented fields in which we planted corn, peas, beans, greens, watermelons, potatoes, sugarcane, and other foods.

Papa taught me basic carpentry – how to hammer nails straight without bending, measure things twice before cutting, saw things evenly, and such. Together on weekends and holidays, we mended fences, chopped firewood, fed chickens, gathered eggs, planted seeds in season, and picked beans and peas, and shucked corn, and such. And on a day in every December, we went into the woods past West Tenth Street and cut down a Red Cedar as a Christmas tree.

When not at work or not fixing things or not tending the fields, Papa sat in his rocking chair on the front porch (often with his mother-in-law) and greeted people who walked past our house (especially children). Papa spoke to a lot of people.

West Fifth Street, an unpaved dirt road without sidewalks, ran east and west, paralleling Kings Road on the north. At the west end, West Fifth Street looped south ninety degrees to end or to begin at Kings Road, depending on which way one was looking. The houses on West Fifth Street faced north or south, depending on which side of the street a house set. Our house was the first house or the last house on the north side of West Fifth Street near the corner of Kings Road, depending on which way one was traveling. Our neighborhood of few automobiles had lots of foot traffic to and from Kings Road, a major, brick-paved highway.

*Kings Road, Florida's first highway, built by the British as the "King's Road" to connect St. Augustine to Colerain, Georgia, passed through the settlement of Cowford (Jacksonville).*

Papa did not spend time at Stamp's Fish Market on Kings Road, the community site where the neighborhood men socialized as they sat on old chairs and boxes in front of Stamp's and watched automobiles travel on Kings Road. The fish market consisted of two, separate, small wooden buildings: a rectangular, glass-fronted space (the store) in which Mr. Stamp sold fresh seafood; and an insulated cubicle (the ice house) from which he sold blocks of ice for the home ice boxes and cold closets in which people kept perishable foods.

Papa was not working as a carpenter when he first met Mama; he was a professional gambler at cards. After marriage and the birth of two of their three children, Felix (my father) and Julius (my aunt), and during Mama's pregnancy with their third child, Huerta, Papa gave up gambling for life, as he promised Mama he would. Mama taught Papa first how to sign his name and later how to read and write.

A vivid vision I have of Mama is her smile whenever she saw Papa, after eating dinner and on his way to sit on the front porch, pick up a newspaper or a magazine to take with him, a newspaper or magazine (Mama had placed strategically and prominently) easily seen and easily reachable.

Papa was just naturally bright, gifted really; he quickly became skilled in any task that he put his mind to. His skills as a gambler and as a carpenter and his grasp of reading and writing without any formal education demonstrated his ability. Mama believed that Papa, when a gambler who could not read or write, developed an unusual capacity for numbers, memorization of odds,

5

frequencies, other mathematical manipulations, and the like. She also believed that Papa's "exceptional natural understanding" of numbers resulted in his "unfortunate natural proficiency" at cards.

Mama repeatedly told the story of Papa and a builder hired by Papa to build a three-bedroom house on property that Papa bought next to our house on West Fifth Street. The story the way Mama told it: After the builder built the house, he gave Papa an itemized bill for the final payment. Papa inspected the house by walking through and around it; he examined the bill; and without use of paper or pencil, he told the builder the board feet of lumber invoiced but not used by the builder in the construction of the house.

Papa worked as a carpenter's helper at the railroad yard outside the city limits of Jacksonville where the railroad kept freight trains. Jim Crow labor practices prevented Papa from working as or receiving the wages of a carpenter. Customarily, due to racial discrimination, skilled Black tradesmen worked as "helpers" to white tradesmen.

Me? Routinely, on a Saturday, when not helping Papa after breakfast, I explored the land beyond West Tenth Street, a wilderness of trees, streams, and animal life, breezes, and smells, always exciting with unexpected and expected dramas of nature.

When waiting for breakfast, I organized the weapons a lone explorer needs during the escapades of the day, my slingshot, and my chinaberry gun. Papa made the chinaberry gun for me. He built the gun from bamboo as the barrel, a glass bottle's neck at the exit end of the bamboo barrel to increase the "pop" sound of a chinaberry when shot from the bamboo barrel, and a decorated shaft carved from a broom handle used to force the chinaberry pellet from the bamboo barrel.

The only chinaberry tree on West Fifth Street grew in our front yard. The tree, old and large, shaded most of the front porch and seasonally yielded hundreds of chinaberries from which I picked ammunition. I stocked my shoulder-mounted ammunition bag with carefully selected chinaberries for my slingshot and of just the right size to exert just the right pressure to shoot smoothly from the bamboo barrel of my chinaberry gun.

This Saturday morning, I started the day as I did every Saturday; I checked the status of breakfast usually served at 8:00 a.m. Cooking odors in the kitchen had squeezed through the wire-weave of the kitchen screen door, swelled as smells, and instantly scattered to skyjack the air of the back porch. Mama was cooking grits with butter and fish roe. The clock in the kitchen showed 7:15 a.m., time enough for me to select my ammunition for the day. I left the back porch to collect chinaberry ammunition.

As I began to climb the chinaberry tree, I heard a scream and Mama call my name. Shock temporarily stunned me; I had never heard Mama raise her voice. I jumped to the ground, ran to the rear of the house, entered the back door, crossed the trellis-latticed back porch to the kitchen screen door, and looked into the kitchen. I saw Mama and Papa facing each other. Papa (180 pounds, six feet tall) loomed over Mama (slender, five feet tall); he was holding Mama's right arm with his left hand; he held his right hand clenched into a fist next to Mama's face. Blue veins crisscrossed Papa's face. Mama, strangely still and quiet, did not seem afraid. The scene surprised, shocked, and confused me, never having heard an angry word spoken between or by either of them. Mama called and referred to Papa as "Mr. Neals." Papa called and referred to Mama as "Sissy" (a reference to how they met). Papa hitting Mama! Unthinkable!

I opened the screen door and ran into the kitchen while shouting, "No Papa!" I grabbed Papa's right wrist; he struggled to get free; and although I did not use all my strength, Papa could not free himself from my grip. He stopped struggling, let go of Mama's arm, and left the kitchen and the house. Mama said to me that everything was "alright," to "go back to playing," and that breakfast would "be ready soon." The kitchen clock showed 7:29 a.m.

Trembling, I left the kitchen and was standing on the back porch trying to decide what to do, when a thought struck me: *I am stronger than Papa.* But that was impossible; no one was stronger than Papa. I remembered walking with Papa when I was younger, he held my hand in his strong hand, as he did and we went to Mr. Stamp's Fish Market to buy fish and block ice. I remembered how "safe" I felt when with Papa, how everyone called him "Mr. Neals." No one called him "Julius," not even Mama. I remembered how "special" I felt because I did not have to call him "Mr. Neals." He was my grandfather, and I called him "Papa."

8

I returned to the front yard and climbed the chinaberry tree. I sat on a high limb and watched Papa slowly hoeing weeds in one of the fields. He looked tired as the eastern sun easily pushed his shadow clockwise across the furrows of the field.

*I am stronger than Papa.*

A thirteen-year-old boy ran into that kitchen. Fourteen minutes later, a teenager stronger than Papa walked out. In fourteen minutes, lifetime changes occurred in me and in my life.

*For the second time, my spirit died and was reborn.*

In the towering chinaberry tree, I sat thinking of what "growing old" was doing to Papa and what "growing up" was doing to me. With each stroke of the hoe, Papa's shadow rose and fell in a silhouette of shade in the heat and light of a vibrant sun.

I sat in the chinaberry tree, staying with Papa until he and his shadow merged with the darkness on the field and became a ghost in the night.

Neither Mama nor Papa ever mentioned the incident to me. I never mentioned the incident to Dad, who lived two blocks from us with Eloise, his wife, and Carol, his daughter; nor did I ever mention the incident to Aunt Julius, who lived across the street from us with her husband, Sam Hezekiah, and their two, beautiful daughters, Cortez Silvia and Carrie Belle, my favorite cousins.

Many-a-day since that Saturday, the last day I climbed the chinaberry tree, I have felt safe and special at sometime in someway because of the man I called "Papa."

Nowadays, I visit my son (Julien X.), his wife (Lauren), and their teenage son (Julien K.), my only grandchild, my grandson whom I call "JK," my grandson who is stronger than I . . . my grandson for whom I never made a chinaberry gun; to whom I never taught basic carpentry, how to drive nails straight without bending, measure twice before cutting, saw things evenly. And together, we never mended fences, chopped firewood, fed chickens or gathered eggs, planted seeds in season, or picked beans and peas or shucked corn; and together, we never walked hand-in-hand to a market to buy fish or ice; and never on a day in a December did we go together into a woods and cut down a Red Cedar tree.

Still, fervently, I hope that at sometime in someway, my grandson has felt "safe" and "special" when with me, the old man whom he calls "Papa."

**Mama.**

Mama, my paternal grandmother, Hattie Cora Brown Neals, as a young woman, was a teacher in a grammar school in a rural town in Georgia (as was her mother, Silvia Brown).

Mama – five feet tall, copper-brown skin, extreme brown eyes always at attention – in early 1900 was the quintessential, cerebral, ingenious, Black woman evolved far ahead of manumission.

To keep her chained to "her place," a subservient place in the human order, her splendidness was brutally snickered, and her valuableness blatantly sniggered, both deliberately.

Even Mama's hygienic lifestyle – her zealous cleanliness of her slender body, the neat, slightly curly, black hair, and the constant washing of her hands that became incessant when she was cooking food – people called an affliction. A lady's salubrity criticized as a malady.

In my moments of anger or conflict, Mama's stated her favorite expression, "Mind!" to remind me to use my mind, to think before acting. With simple words, Mama attempted to have people listen and reason before arguing. Regretfully, her words were often ignored, misunderstood, or ridiculed.

When a schoolteacher in Georgia, Mama's best friend, "Flame," scandalously a "loose woman," worked as a waitress in the "Gut Buckett," the only club for

"Coloreds." It was the public place for music, food, drink, gambling, and other pleasures. Mama's mother forbade Mama from entering the Gut Buckett and from having anything to do with "that Flame person" who was "much too pretty . . . pretty like a fire" and "a living invitation to temptation."

Mama disobeyed her Mother. Mama and Flame enjoyed each other's company. Besides, Mama believed that she was just as pretty as Flame.

One day, Flame excitedly told Mama about a "handsome" new man in town, maybe six feet, 180-190 pounds, wavy black hair in curls about a light complexioned (almost white), clean-shaved face with drowning brown eyes, a strong jaw line, high cheek bones, a long thin nose above a thin-lipped mouth and a square chin – "too handsome for words." His name was "Julius." He was a gambler who played cards every night in the Gut Buckett.

At their clandestine meetings, Flame repeated to Mama the rumors and gossips about the handsome gambler. Each story increased Mama's curiosity and stimulated her imagination. Daily as she went about her day, she looked unsuccessfully to catch a glimpse of the gambler. "He is a 'night person,' " Flame explained. "I've got to see that man," Mama proclaimed.

Mama and Flame made a plan: They chose a night and time when Mama would walk pass the Gut Buckett pass a specific window through which Mama could see the table at which the gambler sat when gambling. Flame would identify the gambler by offering him either food or drink while placing her left hand on his right shoulder. They carried out the plan with feminine efficiency. Without missing a step, Mama walked by the Gut Buckett at the appointed time, saw the gambler, and foresaw love.

With Flame's encouragement and help over the next few months, Mama met and secretively rendezvoused with the gambler, Julius Neals. To disguise any hint of familiarly and to guard against any public slip-of–the-tongue, Mama called and referred to Julius always as "Mr. Neals." It became a habit; she called him Mr. Neals until she died. He called her "Sissy" (because of her restrained lifestyle as a schoolteacher) until he died.

*I believed that "Mr. Neals" and "Sissy" should have been placed in some way on the tombstones. No.*

Late one night, Julius tapped on Mama's bedroom window and told her that he was leaving Georgia "now, right now." He explained that a white man caught cheating during a poker game was killed in a fight. If Mama wanted to be with him, she would have to leave "now, right now." Mama snatched up what clothes she could carry, left a note for her mother, climbed out the window, and left Georgia with Julius.

Mama and Julius married in Florida. In the year 1910, Mama gave birth to a boy, Felix, the first of three children. The gambler-husband became a father; the schoolteacher-wife became a stay-at-home mother. The family's existence depended on Julius's gambling skills. He would arrive home after gambling and from his pockets dump money on the dining room table, or he would come home with empty pockets. Mama developed into a terrific money manager.

Mama taught Julius how to read and write. While pregnant with their third child, a boy (Huerta), Mama confronted Julius: Either the gambling would go, or she and the children would go. Julius promised Mama that he would stop and never gamble again. For the rest of his life, he kept his lifetime promise.

*During my childhood, I heard of Papa's skills at cards and would plead, "Please, Papa. Teach me how to play cards." He always refused, saying, "I promised Sissy."*

Julius used his carpenter skills and worked as a carpenter's helper in the local railroad yard outside the city limits of Jacksonville. He walked the four miles to and from work daily. One day when Julius was leaving to go to work, it was raining. He asked Mama for bus fare to work; she gave him ten cents, the one-way, bus fare. Julius asked for another dime for the bus trip home just in case it was raining when he got off work. Mama told Julius that it would not be raining when he got off work; she had read the weather report in the daily newspaper. Mama was right; it was not raining when he got off work.

Mama read the daily newspapers from front to back every day, although daily newspapers delivered to Negro homes had only one-page of "Negro" news. Mama was an addicted reader.

Mama had an attitude (her "viewpoints") about "important things." The "vote" is the "bloodstream" of freedom. The label on the bottle of success is "sweat." The price of freedom is "knowledge." Mama believed in knowledge and started the education initiative in the family. She stressed the value of education and the worth of knowledge to her children and to the grandchildren whom she lived to know.

Determined, thoughtful, and practical, she dedicated herself to the education of her children. She created ways to "pinch pennies" to help finance the advanced education of her children, one of whom, Huerta Cortez Neals, attended Morehouse, Howard, and Harvard Universities to become a cardiologist. Dr. Neals adopted Mama's vision of an educated family, and he augmented it. He financed and aided in funding the advanced education of three generations of the family.

Mama's children, grandchildren, and great grandchildren include doctors of medicine, of pharmacy, and of education; architect; attorneys; judges; psychologist; social workers; authors; artists; musicians; golfers, and, yes, an accountant/controller of a casino operation.

Mama, proud of her children and grands, would be particularly proud of Carrie Belle (Mama's granddaughter, social worker-analysis) whose love for gambling is well known (and the only person who can clone Mama's fruitcake), and of LaTasha Fifer (Mama's great-granddaughter), the casino official. I convivially picture Mama smiling amusingly at both Carrie Belle and LaTasha while saying coquettishly, "It's in the genes."

Apparently, Mama's mother, Great-Grandmother Brown, forgave Mama for running off unannounced with Papa and marrying him. Mother adored Great-Grandmother Brown, the old, thin, frail woman whom I remember seeing sitting serenely in her special rocking chair on the front porch of the house on West Fifth Street in Jacksonville. She lived there with Mama and Papa until she died.

**The Boy with Bricks.**

The ringing bell reverberates the message throughout the school. School's let out! Three o'clock in the afternoon, "freedom" time. I start the three-mile walk home from Stanton High School, the only high school for Black students in Jacksonville, Florida.

The cemented surfaced streets I walk from school politically and actually stop at the intersection of Myrtle Avenue at West Fifth Street. There, pavement ends and sand begins.

I remove my shoes, leave the jarring pavement of Myrtle Avenue, and step onto the sand of West Fifth Street (my street). The yielding, hot sand zigzags into imprints beneath my feet. My footprints follow me and chart a footpath of my footsteps as I walk on the sandy-side of life.

Smell of pines and sounds of chirps drift in arid air. A warm, encircling breeze shushes me; distantly, behind me, a barely audible voice yells the words, "dummy" and "crazy," words I hear almost every day at some time, at somewhere. A distant voice in an indistinct place does not disrupt my attention to immediate moments in life, hot sand, noises in trees, and crops waving in winds in fields along West Fifth Street.

Unexpectedly, I feel a sharp, hard blow to the back of my head and a warm and wet fluid move down the back of my neck. I touch the pain and find blood on my fingers. I turn, and a few feet behind me stands a boy, smaller (about 5' 9" 140 lbs.) than I (6' 150 lbs.), with bricks in his hands. He sees the blood on my hand, drops the bricks, and runs.

*Acts that intrude on my consciousness annoy me, but do not stir anger or fear. Any interruption in my control over thought interrupts my continuity of existence.*

I pick up the brick with which the boy hit me, take it home, and show it to Mama. She states, "It's not a big brick; you'll live." She suggests that we give the brick a name. "Red. It has your blood on it," she says as she seals the wound with a homemade salve to stop the bleeding and with spider web to prevent infection.

Mama gives me a piece of her homemade fruitcake (my favorite sweet) and sends me out to the fields to gather vegetables for dinner. I linger in the fields and mentally lay out the deed in bits of details until it is hollow, without meaning or mystery.

*I circulate the words and acts of the action through thought until logic renders the incident inconsequential or conceptual. If conceptual, I name the concept for use in distinguishing and associating human behaviors.*

I never saw the boy again. The bricks he left when he ran away, I remove from the road and place in a circle on the roadside. I name each brick and add Red (with my blood still on it) to the circle.

From time to time during walks from school, I stop and talk with Red, Orange, Yellow, Green, Blue, Indigo, and Violet. I repeat the seven stories of the rainbow as told to me by my maternal Great-Grandmother, the dramas and comedies in life of rage, greed, fear, determination, hope, compassion, and love.

Occasionally, through the years, I touch the permanent cranial lump where Red struck my head. I think of rainbows and wonder, *what happened to the abandoned bricks, in particular, Red, with my blood on it.*

Imaginably, the weight of time crushed and entombed the realm of brick and blood into a round grave deep in the sand of West Fifth Street, now lying under the heavily paved, well-maintained, major thoroughfare, "Fifth Street."

**Brown Sub.**

Brown Sub (now Brownsville) in the late 19<sup>th</sup> and early 20<sup>th</sup> centuries was a rural Black community sixteen miles outside Miami city limits on the Everglades side of Florida (a strip of land between the Atlantic Ocean and the Everglades).

The folktale version of how the Wilson family, my material, great grandparents, settled there: The eras of enslavement in Florida of Black people and the Seminole Wars coincided. Osceola (a Seminole war leader) raided white settlements and encouraged enslaved Black men to flee enslavement and join the Seminole fight. Word of Osceola's raids quickly spread; Blacks, free and fugitive, male and female, sought sanction in the Everglade. The Blacks who joined with bands of Seminole Native Americans in the Everglades were called "Black Seminoles."

*Three separate cultures coexisted in the Everglades: Seminole Native American people, free Blacks and fugitive Blacks (Maroons) people, and integrated Seminole and Black peoples.*

A man called "Wilson," a fugitive from enslavement, fled to the Everglades where he lived among Seminole Native Americans and Black Seminoles. After the Emancipation Proclamation, Wilson left the Everglades with his wife and children. He and other freedmen homesteaded land sixteen miles south of Miami in a Black settlement called "Brown's Sub," later known as "Brown Sub."

In 1936, after my parents' divorce, Mother and I moved to Brown Sub to live with Mother's Grandmother (my maternal Great-Grandmother), Della Thomas, in the home of Mother's father (my maternal Grandfather), the Reverend Joseph Wilson (Papa Wilson), a Bishop of the African Methodist Episcopal Church in Southern Florida.

Great-Grandmother Thomas's daughter, Lylia (my mother's mother), was Papa Wilson's first wife; she died when Mother (also named Lylia) and Mother's younger sister and only sibling, Altamese, were toddlers. Great-Grandmother Thomas reared Mother and Altamese.

Papa Wilson's adjacent neighbors in Brown Sub were all Wilson family members: Altamese Wilson Shipp Brown Brown (Aunt Alta); Julia Wilson, Papa Wilson's only sister (Grandaunt Julia); Granduncles Fred Wilson and Charlie Wilson (Papa Wilson's brothers), spouses, and cousins. Family members owned and lived on adjourning acres combined into a Wilson land-bloc.

At age seven, I wandered alone on Wilson land without hearing ominous and deterring "no's" and "don'ts's." Family, aware of my behavior "differences" (being "touched") knew that I would not voluntarily leave Wilson land. Even so, family members closely and continuously "watched-over" and "checked-on" me. I was Lylia's "only child" and Reverend Wilson's "only grandchild." Relatives supplied a pony-express child-watch service that kept Mother and other family members aware of my movements, where I was, what I was doing, and in which direction I was going. When wandering alone within land and time limits and family caring attention, I felt safe, special, and free, not caged for my "own sake" or my "own good."

I walked raw evolving land with evolving life: Plants with razor sharp foliage and flowers grew there. Snakes, scorpions, butterflies, grasshoppers, jackrabbits, birds, bees, wasps, spiders, ants, and other wildlife lived there.

Sounds were there, everywhere. Hums and clicks in grass, rustles and chatter in bushes, chirps and caws in trees. In the sky, wings swooshed, and winds whistled. Rhythms gave the addresses of places.

Food, plentiful and free, grew wild and in groves. I freely choose what, when, and where to eat. I ate from roots, vines, plants, and trees – papayas, potatoes, carrots, tomatoes, raw honey, watermelons, mangoes, oranges, apples, cantaloupes, peaches, bananas, pomegranates, and coconuts.

The uniqueness of coconuts amazed me, the taste of the pulp and the water and the way a coconut grew a coconut palm tree. A coconut fell to the ground, and if left alone, it rooted and sprouted a palm tree, but I could still eat the meat inside the coconut. Alone in nature, I did as told: I left nature alone and watched as nature worked (what Great-grandmother Thomas called) "miracles."

Papa Wilson taught me how to shell and open a coconut using the sharp flanges of Oolite limestone rock found on the land. Also for me, he built a rope swing on a limb of one of the rubber trees near the big house, the house in which we lived.

Grand Mother Thomas made chewing gum by mixing syrup and sap from a rubber tree. She also made hardrock candy out of syrup. I disliked the syrup, the gum, and the candy. I liked to chew the natural sap of a rubber tree when singing while swinging on my swing. Papa Wilson taught me how to be careful of mites and crickets when tapping a rubber tree for sap-gum.

If I were late in returning home from a fantasy safari, Mother would scold me about the dangers on the land. Neither Mother nor any relative ever hit me, regardless of my behavior. If any physical danger existed to me on Wilson land, it was not from people. Mother explained using reason. She warned of restricting me to the yard of the big house if I did not get home before dark. The thought of such a restriction terrified me.

If weather or any event kept me within the house, I played alone with my marbles and my blanket. I tossed the blanket into the air and let it fall to lie on the floor. The blanket's uneven surface became a stage with plains, hills, and valleys – places I populated with marbles of beautiful colors envisaged as people. I created a civilization, generated a culture, and staged a humanity in which I played a major part.

Frequently, I became so immersed in dramatic play that I refused to stop to eat or to sleep. Mother worried.

One day, to get me out of the house to play with relatives' children, Mother took my marbles from me. I quickly realized that I did not need marbles. Without marbles, the blanket distracted the movement of my thought. The loss of need for use of both marbles and blanket erased my reliance on generic externals (so easily taken away) and liberated my vision from me to people, people to person, and person to me.

*I live within me with me, a person, not a people. Without me live persons, not a people. Humanity is persons, not a people. The heart of humanity is a person, not a people.*

I lived in Brown Sub with Mother until my father kidnapped me when I was ten years old. One morning without Mother's knowledge, he removed me from an elementary school class in Brown Sub and took me to Jacksonville; there I lived with my paternal grandparents until the summer after my sixteenth birthday.

On a vividly clear day, June 7, I left family to extend my walk to lands beyond Jacksonville and Brown Sub. I enlisted in the Army of the United States.

## Aunt Altamese and Husbands.


Aunt Alta (Altamese Wilson Shipp Brown Brown), my mother's younger sister and only sibling, was not a small woman. She referred to her 200 pounds packed proportionately into a five-foot, six-inch tall, shapely, amply curved body as "pleasing plump." Men agreed. Her large, hazel eyes reflected a constant state of expectancy while looking at life and complimented her round, medium-brown face, and full lips. Her nappy, short, black hair refused to obey any hairstyle. Aunt Alta did not easily disappear into a crowd and never wanted to.

As a young woman, Aunt Alta was taught how to shoot a revolver and received a "thirty-eight special" pistol as a gift from a local policeman who was "sweet" on her. She purse-packed the thirty-eight. Her reputation, "fearless." She used a right hand with only two fingers and part of a thumb to fire the gun. She was an excellent shot.

When a small child, Aunt Alta picked up a bright red object that exploded in her right hand, blowing off most of her middle and index fingers and part of her thumb. The explosion also affected her sight; she wore eye glasses all her life. The object was a high explosive, homemade firecracker; the occasion was the fourth of July. The event shaped Aunt Alta's life; she was a living firecracker and lived every day as if it were the fourth of July.

Aunt Alta lived her entire life on land given to her by Papa Wilson. Her land bordered the properties of Papa

Wilson and Grandaunt Julia.

Aunt Alta and her first husband, (Uncle) Leonard Shipp, physically matched. He was five feet seven inches tall with 200 pounds. He was Geechee, spoke Gullah, and had a slight stutter. Come to think of it, Aunt Alta's husbands (whom I knew) often stuttered a bit when they talked with her.

Uncle Leonard worked as a chef at a hotel on Miami Beach. He drove a large, 4-door, Chevrolet sedan to work. Uncle Leonard kept blankets, snacks, and other comforts in the rear seat of the car for resting and taking naps during breaks at his job. The hotel's facility for workers was a "white-only" employee lounge.

Aunt Alta did not believe that Uncle Leonard used the blankets and other items only for resting at work; she was certain that he had an "outside woman," and the items had "other uses."

Habitually, after arriving home from work, Uncle Leonard would take a bath and lounge around the house or go to a local bar in Brown Sub. Sometimes, on a Saturday, he would dress and drive into Colored Town in Miami to "drink and gamble in clubs with cronies and fool around with some hussy," according to Aunt Alta.

*After incorporation of Miami as a city is 1896, "Colored Town" (now Overtown) was so termed to define that part of Miami settled by railroad, Black construction workers. The history of Miami notes that of the 362 men who voted to incorporate Miami as a city, 168 voters are identified as "colored."*

26

During an evening after work (not a Saturday), Aunt Alta noticed that Uncle Leonard used an unusually big amount of Old Spice cologne during his after-work bath routine. She became suspicious when he said that he was driving into Colored Town "to play cards with the guys."

Uncle Leonard was still dressing when Aunt Alta put her 38 into her purse, got into Uncle Leonard's car, lay on the rear floor next to the back seat, and covered herself with the car blankets.

Uncle Leonard, relieved at not seeing Aunt Alta as he was leaving the house, drove away in a hurry. In Colored Town, he picked up a young woman whom he greeted with "sweet words" (as told by Aunt Alta). He parked in the parking lot of the one "hotel" (a two-story rooming house) in Colored Town. Uncle Leonard and the woman went into the hotel.

Aunt Alta waited a few minutes, got out of the car, and entered the hotel. She asked the desk clerk, "What room is Leonard in?"

The clerk replied with pretended surprise. "Leonard? I don't remember the last time I saw Leonard."

From her purse, Aunt Alta pulled the 38, cocked it, and asked again, "What room is Leonard in?"

The clerk told Aunt Alta the room number, offered her a key to the room, and left the hotel.

Aunt Alta found the room, and opened the door with her

shoulder, surprising Uncle Leonard and the woman, whom Aunt Alta told in creative terms what would happen to her if she "fool around with Leonard again." Uncle Leonard reached for his clothes; Aunt Alta shot a bullet into the bed near him.

With gun drawn, Aunt Alta paraded a naked Uncle Leonard out of the hotel, through the street and parking lot, and to the car. Naked Uncle Leonard drove the car from Colored Town to Brown Sub. From then on, his nickname was "Old Spice." Soon after, Aunt Alta and Uncle Old Spice divorced.

Aunt Alta's second husband, (Uncle) Oscar Brown, was a bit younger than she. Good looking, dark complexioned, medium build, and six feet tall, he smiled all the time. People said that Uncle Oscar had "real pretty white teeth" and had a lot to smile about, "New off the boat" from the islands and with "no regular job" (said politely), with "no job" (said truthfully), he landed free room and board with a woman who "loved him."

Uncle Oscar had heard the Old Spice story; he wore cologne (not Old Spice) all the time. He was athletic, and that was good; it served him well one evening.

Uncle Oscar worked as a construction laborer. He occasionally worked (said politely); he seldom worked (said truthfully). Aunt Alta worked a six-day week as a nursing assistant at Jackson Memorial Hospital, the only local hospital that accepted Black patients.

Uncle Oscar had most days free and was always neatly dressed in colorful pants and a tropical-patterned shirt.

He entertained many of his friends from the Bahamas on Aunt Alta's front porch. The daily gathering became a ritual; people came and went freely.

Aunt Alta said that she just got "sick and tired" of Oscar treating her with "no respect" like a "low fence" or a "crumb." His "no-good so-called friends" walk onto her property, sit on her front porch, and eat her food and drink her liquor "whenever they felt like it." What she really hated was all those people using her bathroom.

Aunt Alta had a six-foot high fence with a locking front gate built around the house. She forbade Uncle Oscar from entertaining anyone at her house when she was not home. Uncle Oscar's answer to Aunt Alta's fence with the locking gate was to take his social gatherings elsewhere, to the house of an "outside woman," so Aunt Alta heard.

To Aunt Alta's questions about his suspected affair, Uncle Oscar accused her of "sniffin' 'round" into his "bisness" and that she "just might find somethin' " if she kept "sniffin'." That was a mistake. An argument led to an in-your-face argument during which Uncle Oscar shouted angrily to Aunt Alta, "You drive me to other woman!" That, too, was a mistake.

Aunt Alta headed for her bedroom. Uncle Oscar headed for the front door; he knew where she kept her 38. Before Aunt Alta could get off a shot, Uncle Oscar reached the front porch, and in an enormous hurdle cleared the six-foot high fence with inches to spare.

Aunt Alta sniffed around among Uncle Oscar's things in

the house, found incriminating stuff, and threw everything of his over the fence and onto the dirt street. Friends of Uncle Oscar picked up his things from the street. After the divorce, I sometimes saw (ex-uncle) Oscar in Colored Town. He was smiling. He did have real pretty white teeth.

A few years later, Aunt Alta married another man named Brown. I did not get to know that (Uncle Brown #2) man. I talked briefly with him at Aunt Alta's funeral. He and I agreed: When it came to life, Aunt Alta "turned it out."

Aunt Alta was childless and without a niece or any other nephew. She liked being a Wilson in Brown Sub. In Brown Sub on Wilson land, she was born, lived, died, and buried. At her death, the only cemetery in Brown Sub for burial of the black dead consisted entirely of land donated to the Brown Sub community by her father, the Reverend Joseph Wilson.

Aunt Alta, you are at home, a Wilson in Wilson land.

Aunt Alta, stand down; cease fire.

## What's A Jew?

The two simultaneous explosions – the blast of light from the electric light bulbs in the ceiling of the room and the shouts of the Staff Sergeant – awake every one of the 63 men housed in the army barrack on the cantonment center of Camp Stoneman

"Up! This is what you've been waitin' for! Pack everything and fall out in twenty minutes. You're shippin' out. You're goin' to go on an ocean voyage on an army cruise ship. Twenty minutes!"

*I was in the Army happily. I volunteered. People who knew me were surprised that the army accepted me. "That crazy boy is going to the army?" Their surprise surprised me.*

Twenty minutes would be time enough. Our Black infantry company arrived at the 2,841.54-acre cantonment center of Camp Stoneman in Pittsburg, California, a month ago and, as ordered, maintained readiness by "being on standby." "Being on "standby" meant "be ready to be shipped out anytime, twenty-four seven." At our arrival at Camp Stoneman, the white officers stated the average stay before deployment was "three days," then "four or five days," and then "one to two weeks." Military Black personnel at the camp privately told us the deployment of Black troops always took longer than for white troops. They did not say why. I believed the probable cause was racial segregation. Black soldiers had to fit within the availability of racially segregated facilities, in America, on the ocean, and overseas; any disruption in the movement anywhere of

Black troops affected deployment of Black-troop somewhere.

I read in a military bulletin that the first military unit to embark from Camp Stoneman to the Pacific Theater was a Black field artillery regiment from Harlem, New York. The information is educational and revealing, especially when noted with persistent rumors of the use of Black military personnel as guinea pigs in experiments.

At seventeen years old and in California for the first time, I am glad for the deployment delay. Pittsburg sits at the junction of two rivers, the Sacramento and the San Joaquin (a waterway to San Francisco Bay). There are waterways, highways, and railways that take me the 40 miles northeast to San Francisco and to the elating black community in Oakland. I excitedly and untiringly rejoice in an America I had not known or heard of before.

In Oakland, I felt my first teenage love, thrilling, innocent love with the curvaceous, tall, honey brown, exquisite Anita; Anita with inquiring oval eyes and inquisitive full lips. I think of her as I pack my ditty bag in Camp Stoneman for the last time (I thought).

Within the twenty minutes, we evacuate the khaki colored barracks and line up with army gear in the damp, chilly, foggy, Camp Stoneman morning. This roll call is very different from previous assemblies. The usual jokes, the "Your-mama" replies, and the hyena-laughs are AWOL.

Each soldier stands quietly at ease, waiting for his name to be called, to climb aboard a troop truck for transport through the portals inscribed, "Through these Portals Pass the Best Damn Soldiers in the World" to the Pittsburg Waterfront to make a four-hour ferry trip to Fort Mason, San Francisco Port of Embarkation. There, at Pier 15 or Pier 45, board a ship for a destination somewhere in the Pacific Theater. Impatiently, I wait. This would be my first ocean voyage.

The attentive silence of the soldiers on the field is methodically hyphenated by the call of a name and a response. While listening for my name to be called, I mentally recall the stories told repeated throughout our cantonment.

*The shooting war in the Pacific is officially over, and the American troops who won that war are returning home. We, the new troops standing at the ready, are being deployed either to Japan to serve under Emperor-General Douglas MacArthur or to Pacific Islands to clear caves, mountains, forests, and jungles of Japanese soldiers who refuse to surrender, because of orders not to surrender or of the samurai code of Bushido, death over surrender. I didn't know my destination. Rumors were notoriously unreliable.*

The deployment procedure ends. The last transport truck leaves the compound. One soldier stands alone waiting on the field – Me.

*I think of an old saying, "Many are called, but few are chosen." Ok. But now what?*

A white First Lieutenant approaches me. "Neals?"

"Yes, Sir," I reply while saluting.

He returns my salute. "You're not being deployed."

"Why not, Sir?"

He seems as confused as I. "A shipping code withdrew your name from the deployment list. Return to your barrack and wait for further orders."

This day is strange. White officers seldom speak directly to an individual, enlisted soldier below a certain rank; that is the job of Black non-coms (non-commissioned officers).

I return to the barrack. During the day, I leave twice briefly, for breakfast and lunch at the mess hall. I am reading in the barrack when a white officer, a Major, enters. I stand up at attention and salutes.

"You Neals?" he asks as he returns my salute.

"Yes, Sir," I answer while thinking, *Today is my day for white officers. Unusual, unusually good or unusually bad. I am curious but not concerned. I am in the Army.*

"At ease, Neals." Handing me a document, the Major says, "This is an order for you to report for training tomorrow at 08:00 at the administration building listed in the order. Show the order to the guard on duty at the admin building."

"Training, Sir?" My voice expresses my surprise.

"Yes. Hold questions for now. Unpack; choose a bunk in this barrack. You will be housed here temporarily. All other soldiers housed in this barrack will be in a readiness cycle for deployment in a few days. Logistics make any development of a close relationship unlikely between you and any another soldier housed here.

*I think the officer's statement about a "close relationship" odd. A thin smile on the officer's face tells me that he knows that it what I am thinking.*

He turns to leave; I salute. His response is more of an arm gesture towards the front door where he is headed than a returned salute.

I read the information written on the document, a single 8 ½" x 11" sheet marked "Confidential." The order number 13 identifies me by RA (Regular Army) number, not by name, the administration building by number and location, and the training class as "MOS" (military occupation specialty), "Information and Education."

*Never heard of it, did not know what it meant or why I needed further training. I received extensive training in Fort Benning, Georgia, and in Aberdeen Proving Ground, Maryland.*

At 07:55 hours the next day, Wednesday, I enter the designated administration building; give the order to a guard who hands the order to a lieutenant sitting at a desk displaying a "Duty Officer" sign. He has me sit while he makes a telephone call. Shortly, the Major appears who had spoken to me at the barrack.

"Follow me, Neals."

I follow the Major down a hall and up steps to a second-floor doorway, a locked, solid-metal door inscribed, "Restricted Area." The Major unlocks the door, and we enter a large space. He gestures for me to look around.

Space, all-inclusive of the second floor and windowless is sectioned into areas by glass walls. The first section nearest the entrance encloses a classroom containing numbered, mobile desk-chairs with a writing arm, electronic blackboards, tables, and other equipment. The other sections hold a variety of instruments, including computers, arms and weapons, and a library. Most of the materials, equipment, arms, and weapons I was unaware existed.

The Major (later introduced as Major Baker, the officer in charge of the operation) enters the classroom, sits at a desk in the last row and gestures for me to sit at the desk next to him. I do so. He turns towards me.

*He personifies the Army officer pictured on posters: White, physically fit body, closely cut, light brown hair, penetrating blue eyes, with everything else forming squares or rectangles; his posture, unyielding.*

"As you see, we are the first ones here. The other soldiers will be arriving at 0900. I want to explain this situation to you first. Once I explain, you have a choice; you can say 'no' to being part of this unit without any punishing consequences. You understand?"

"Yes, Sir."

"Good. Most of what I am telling you will be told to the group. You, first, because you are the only Negro soldier in the group of 13. The other 12 soldiers are white teenagers, 18 or 19 years old. You are the youngest at 17. Individually, you will train together and nothing else; not during training; not after completion of training; you will not work together on missions. This rule will be strictly followed. Any disobedience will cause immediate disciplinary action. Understand?"

"Yes, Sir. No problem here. I'm a Southerner, lived in only Negro communities, went to only Negro schools, served in only Negro army units."

"No!" The Major exclaims shaking his head. "That's not what I mean."

The entry door to the room opens. A Captain and a Master Sergeant enter the facility. Both seem surprised to see the Major sitting and talking with me. They greet him.

"Good Morning, Major."

"Good Morning, Sir."

"Good Morning, Captain. Sergeant."

The Major continues his explanation. "The rule of separation may seem extreme, but we think it is necessary to ensure anonymity and to safeguard the existence of all involved. Each soldier in the unit of thirteen will be known only by a number, not by name. The unit is Baker Boy Special Operation Unit. In Baker

Boy Unit, your number is 13, Baker Boy 13 or BB 13. The decision to add a Negro soldier to the unit was made after formation of the twelve-man unit, an afterthought in anticipation (of what some military leaders believe is) an inevitable future. Perhaps you have heard of or read recently the FBI's report about Japan's Black Dragon Society's subversive efforts to influence Black Nationalist organizations in America."

"Yes, Sir. I read about it in a couple of Negro newspapers."

"Does the number '13' bother you?"

"No, Sir."

"From your records, I didn't think it would.

"This unit is established to meet a changing world resulting from the war, such as changes in global territories, political and religious authorities, aims and priorities. We are in a war after the war; a war to win minds and politically overturn governments began long before the shooting war ended.

"The winners in this unannounced 'third world war,' will possess sovereign world power, and not necessarily be nations as known today. America's place as a world power is not assured or promised. The Baker-Boy mission is to ensure for Americans our country's present and future status as a free global power."

As the Major talks, the Captain and the Master Sergeant place materials and equipment in sections of the space.

At 0845, the master sergeant leaves the facility. He returns in about ten minutes with a group of young, white soldiers; he instructs the soldiers:

"On your orders is a number, 1 through 13. That's your ID in the unit, and the only way you will be known to anyone in the unit, as Baker Boy, or BB 1 to BB 13. Your ID is also your desk number. On the double! Find your desk and take a seat!"

The soldiers look for the assigned desks. The Major stands and says to me, "Give it all you've got." He joins the Captain and the Master Sergeant at the front of the classroom. I realize I am sitting at desk 13.

The Master Sergeant greets us: "This is the Baker Boy Unit, and you are Baker Boys. Good morning, Baker Boys!"

In unison, we reply, "Good morning, Master Sergeant!"

The Master Sergeant turns to and salutes Major Baker. "Sir. Baker Boy unit all present."

"Thank you, Master Sergeant." Major Baker carefully looks at each of us seated in the room. "You obviously have questions.

"First, the name of the unit, 'Baker Boy Special Operation Unit.' It is a parody. I am Major Baker, command leader; thirteen, the total number of you, is a baker's dozen. The name is not imitative of 'Baker Street Irregulars' that appear in Sherlock Holmes stories as the name of a troop of street kids who work as intelligence agents, nor is it copied from the British secret intelligence unit also known as 'Baker Street Irregulars.'

"What about you? Look around. Each soldier you see is a soldier 17, 18, or 19 years old, who, as far as the Army knows, is someone you do not know, have never met or seen before today.

"Why you? Why are you here? You are here because civilian and army records tell the same stories. Each of you volunteered for military service when you graduated high school; you chose to be here, to serve your country; and so far, you have done so, willingly and openly.

"Records profile you as secretive and private, with little or no interest in having a close relationship with other people. You prefer to work alone; you go for perfection in your actions, no matter how many times you must do something over and over. In fact, you like repetition. You excel in whatever you do when you want to. We know that usually you are considered and treated as 'odd' or 'crazy, even 'mentally retarded.' Each of you has extraordinary abilities, and you excel in using your skills, especially during adversity. Also, you are young and, hopefully, without a fixed allegiance to what you have been told so far as truth and morality in today's world.

Those and other traits you have are attributes we look for in select individuals. These qualities, we think, will allow you to receive and accept the training required and to serve as needed in an assigned mission.

"Yes. We used pieces of paper to help us make the crucial decision to bring you here for this critical mission, to tell you that your country wants the 'you' imprinted on paper, to say to you, we can train you to be a formidable force in service to your country. To promise you that future references to you will not be 'mental retard' or 'crazy,' or any other such related term."

The Major's change in attitude shows in his change of posture, to almost an "at-attention" position.

"World War II is called the first 'high-tech war.' The war for the peace is the real 'high-tech war.' The American standards of life, health, safety, and welfare of its people as a world power are threaten, and survival will depend on the immediate commitment of our government to develop technologies and techniques to anticipate, prevent, and defeat intimidations and imminent attacks on democracy internally and externally by individuals, groups, and nations.

"Nations and groups will compete in intermediate races using limited violence, threats of atoms, hydrogen, uranium, missiles, and technology. The final race will be won by the intelligent human use of artificial intelligence and robotic technology.

"Why the cloak-and-dagger approach to this mission? There are powers within our country that do not realize, or for political reasons, do not admit either that a third world war for global dominance has begun or that America is unprepared. The concepts, ideologies, methods, equipment, and weapons of the past are useless in the battles to be fought in this war, domestic and foreign. We must prepare and be able to do whatever is necessary to protect our country from all who would destroy it in any name – war, peace, freedom, racism, religion, multiculturalism, automation, etcetera – including well-intentioned, but misled citizens, whatever the citizens' social, economic, political or government membership or status. Government and mainstream citizens are wrong about the peace as they are wrong about you. Government has prematurely ordered the dissolution of this country's safeguards. A blatant example is the Office of Strategic Services. Government has scheduled OSS for termination as superfluous! And the people do nothing."

The Major pauses, takes a deep breath, and quietly says, "We must make every effort to prevent or neutralized all such future, destructive, political action. To be effective as a small group, it is leaderships that we must influence."

Again, the Major pauses before continuing. "We are committed to prepare you thoroughly for this mission and to do whatever is necessary and possible to protect you from political, economic, social or physical interference or harm to you because of your involvement in this mission. If the mission and your participation became public knowledge, there could and probably would be severe, even life-threatening consequences from powerful groups and influential persons. There are without doubt groups and persons of whom we are unaware who would vigorously oppose this mission. To carry out this mission, we will fight known and unknown adversaries.

"Our cloak-and-dagger method structures anonymity as deep as possible as a first line of defense to shield you against penalties for patriotic actions in unpatriotic times. I repeat, 'we are committed.' Your commitment must be as ours, without reservation, total, unquestionable, and uncompromising.

"How, where, and what are you to do? The how's where's and what's will be trained over two, eight-week training phases by an international cadre of instructors, American and foreign.

"Your training began today when you walked into this room. Words used and ideas and concepts presented to you were deliberate. Get familiar with them. Use the resources of this facility, the library, other equipment, and study sessions held by your instructors. All your instructors are subject-matter experts. I promise you. Master the language of concepts, ideologies, and political and military tactics and strategies we teach, and you will change mentally, emotionally, educationally, and physically and never again fear the call 'mental retard.' This special unit for special people is your unit. You are special people.

"In sixteen weeks, the 'you' you see in a mirror will be a 'special you,' not the 'you' you see today in glass or read about today on paper."

Again, the Major stops talking and looks at each of us. Exhilarated, appreciative, and filled with anticipation of my future, I am impatient for whatever is next.

Major Baker, "Anyone wants to leave do it now."

Only heads and eyes move.

Major Baker: "Your formal instruction starts tomorrow 0900 hours. Your first instructor is a Jew, a partisan from the Middle East. Any specific questions ask now."

I raise my hand.

"Yes, BB 13?"

"Sir. What's a Jew?"

## The Making of BB 13.

Made it! I completed the Baker Boy Special Operations training at Camp Stoneman.

We, Baker Boys, were "Military Occupational Specialists. Information and Education." We did not get a document or an insignia to record the occasion. Major Baker stated how proud he was (and how proud our country would be) of us, as he shook hands with each of us. I accepted his words. I believed him. He clarified my cause for being a cause of being for my country. I entrusted him with my future, my life.

He kept his promise: Today's "I am" is not yesterday's "me." Today I am unconcerned with the past, and labels, such as "mental retard," mean nothing.

My base assignment appears to be a perfect placement for me. My IA (individual augmentee) deployment orders me to augment a "Negro" transport unit as a military vehicle driver in the Pacific Theater. The objective of the placement is to give me freedom of movement where constant travel is normal conduct, and my absences from the base should not ordinarily arouse suspicion.

My travel documents include a special, heavily laminated permanent pass: It authorizes me, Corporal Neals, unlimited travel in the Pacific Theater.

The day arrives (my thoughts play like a broken record). I travel through the portals – "Through these Portals Pass the Best Damn Soldiers in the World" – to the Pittsburg

Waterfront and ferried for four hours to Fort Mason, San Francisco Port of Embarkation, US Army; at the 650-foot long Pier 15, I board a Liberty ship.

I anchor my excitement of my first-ocean-voyage when I hear that the ship is docked for the night and scheduled to leave tomorrow at a slack-water time.

I settle in at my hammock and go up to the main deck. Leaning on the ship's railing, I look at the early lights of Oakland and think of Anita. Where is Anita now? At home? Thinking of me? Or helping in the Oakland bar owned by her mother? (Another broken-record thought) I think of Anita as always: "My first teenage love, thrilling, innocent love with the curvaceous, tall, honey brown, exquisite Anita; Anita with inquiring oval eyes and inquisitive full lips." I wonder if we will meet again.

Bugled retreat sounds over the water; 16:30 hours. I throw a kiss towards the Oakland lights and mouths, "Goodnight; goodbye." I salute in the direction of Camp Stoneman. I feel complete. I am in the Army; I am a special person. I stand resolved, ready to kill and to die for my America – well trained to do one, well prepared to do the other, and willing to do both.

Impatient for my first ocean voyage to begin, I walk the decks where permitted. As I walk, I think about the other Baker Boys and their assignments, whatever and wherever. Our situation is exceptional. I know every other B Boy well in many ways that relate to the value of each to the mission, physically and mentally, their strengths, limitations, preferences, and idiosyncrasies. However, after training together, we parted without my

46

knowing the other B Boys. I do not know the true personal brand of anyone – names, hometowns, educational institutions, experiences, families, passions (outside of military), prior military units or training, personal associations, and memories. Major Baker wanted it that way for our "protection," he said.

I believe that the other B Boys, all white soldiers, obeyed Major Baker's anonymity orders. A Black soldier, I was quartered in segregated facilities in a segregated area. I saw and associated with the other B Boys only during actual training sessions, never before or after.

The bugle call of taps sounds the 2200 hour. I retire to my hammock to roam freely in sleep.

A white officer, Captain Ball, commands the black transportation company I reported to on Sand Island. I am told that the Captain was briefed about my "special military status" in the unit, my standing order to obey a mission assignment immediately as a direct order of top priority, and that an assignment could require me to take leave from the company suddenly and for unspecified duration of time. I am directed to inform the Captain of the date and time of a leave of absence before I leave the Pacific military base.

It is evident at the time of my arrival; Captain Ball resents having a soldier in the company over whom he does not have complete control. The Captain's reaction is to assign me as leader of a squad.

As squad leader, I am responsible and accountable for the welfare and the conduct of all squad members, many of whom routinely complain and report to me right-to-life issues – blatant discrimination in work assignments, leave time, and health (sick call).

Sick call means seeing a black medical orderly at a company barrack, not a doctor or anyone at the field hospital unless death appears imminent.

Leave time off base for Black soldiers is usually approved during weekdays. Race riots frequently occur on weekends between Black and white military personnel on leave off military bases; consequently, off base leave on the weekend is primarily reserved for white troops.

Addressing issues of squad members demands extensive durations of my time, and being accountable for the behavior of squad members, even when I am away on BB assignments, causes numerous confrontations with Captain Ball. The Captain reacts with punishments of me: Written reprimands, a summary court-martial, and a reduction in rank from sergeant to corporal.

Two years in the company do not improve the relationship between the Capitan and me. I am privately alerted that he is preparing a request for an Article 32 hearing to consider having a Court-Martial Convening Authority convene a special or general court-martial against me, based on a record of violations of duties (primarily absences without leave). Captain Ball is not privy to any particular facts about my BB assignments, but, I am sure, he knows that regulations prohibit me from revealing any information concerning BB activities. Essentially, in a court-martial proceeding, I would be defenseless.

I suspect that the Captain made recent inquiries concerning my "special military status," and not finding a military source to either deny or confirm, he decides to see if I were "fair game."

I also have other concerns. Over my thirty months of service, numerous changes have occurred in the military-industrial complex and national and military leaders and politics. I do not know if any of the changes affect me personally. For the last four months, I have not received a BB assignment.

An enlisted soldier with less than six months until eligibility for discharge, I know I may apply for a transfer to a stateside army base to serve the remainder of my enlistment term. Not knowing the procedure by which to apply for the transfer, I ask the advice of a Black soldier (from my home state of Florida) who is a clerk in Battalion Headquarters. He tells me, according to my military record, I am ineligible for the six-month transfer provision because of the number of furloughs I have taken. And, yes, he has heard the rumor that a court-martial and imprisonment in the stockade at Schofield Barracks are pending possibilities for me.

My records need immediate correction. That is possible but only plausible if a transfer order simultaneously and instantaneously occurs, thereby not giving Captain Ball time in which to react in a retraction of the order. I broke protocol; I asked for help and got it. It came with an unusually worded message that I did not understand. "Thank you. Safe trip. Goodbye." In three weeks, I was aboard a ship scheduled for Fort Mason, San Francisco, California. My final destination was Fort Eustis, Newport

News, Virginia, to await discharge.

As the ship weigh anchor, I realize that I momentarily stopped breathing as I waited for the ship's departure. I take a full breath of air and begin to breathe again. I decide then that I will use the 72-hour layover at Camp Stoneman before transport to Fort Eustis to search for answers about Baker Boy Operation Unit. I hope that I will discover knowledge that medicates my stress and inoculates me against anxiety.

As I pass the California sign, "Welcome Home. Well Done." posted along the route from Fort Mason to Camp Stoneman, I respond, "Thank you. Had a safe trip. Goodbye."

Camp Stoneman had housed German and Italian prisoners of war. Consequently, I exercise caution when asking questions about army military personnel and operations.

I appear in Camp Stoneman as I appeared on military assignments. Just another Black-soldier, seen, but unnoticed and ignored, a baggage-handler, porter, waiter, janitor, bartender, chauffeur in situations and locations more precarious than Camp Stoneman. Another "Negro soldier," one of many soldiers back from overseas asking for help to reconnect with military colleagues. The White officer in battalion headquarters is sympathetic and tries to help me in my search.

There is no "Major Baker" registered on any of the rosters that record the 125 officers permanently assigned to Camp Stoneman at any one time. Neither

50

"Baker Boy" nor "Military Occupational Specialist" is listed among the 16, permanent, training resources based at Camp Stoneman. Available (unclassified) training documents do not refer to a "Military Occupational Specialist" title, or to a "Baker Boy Special Operation Unit." The administration building that contained the BB training facility is now a secured warehouse. Standing in front of the warehouse, I get an "aha" moment.

*The only name I know of any person associated with the Baker Boy Special Operation Unit is "Major Baker." The name, "Major Baker," is probably a "parody," as "Major Baker" called "Baker Boys" a "parody." Everything about the operation was "major," a major undertaking; a major experiment of using a baker's dozen of teenage soldiers with mental issues and extraordinary abilities; a major play on words with words by "Major Baker" to affect major transformations militarily, politically, and socially, including a major change in my life. "Thank you, 'Major Baker.'"*

I leave for Fort Eustis.

Relaxed in Fort Eustis, I envisage discharge on June 6, the prescribed termination date of my enlistment term. That does not happen. I presume "problem" and wait for an attack by an "unknown combatant."
Inexplicably, on June 8, I receive my honorable discharge in the regular course of administrative procedure. The explanation for the delay, "Retained in Sv 2 days for the conv of the govt."

Years later, I obtain a copy of my army records and learn

that I had been partially "sheep dipped." A large sum of information is missing from my military records. The training I completed in Fort Benning, Georgia, in Aberdeen Proving Ground, Maryland, and in Camp Stoneman, California is not accurately recorded. The medical history does not note my illnesses of malaria and jungle rot (body rash), nor the two operations performed on my left hand. In fact, there is no medical history in the records, not even of vaccinations. The only training entry is military truck driver. My promotion to sergeant and the reduction in rank to corporal are unrecorded. Army records report: I served in military service, was awarded a WW II Pacific Theater service medal, and received an honorable discharge.

After viewing my military records, I partly understand the words of the last message I received as BB 13: "Thank you. Safe trip. Goodbye." The Baker Boy operation was over. My military record was probably manipulated for multiple reasons, not just to extract me from a situation, but, more importantly, to control any release of information about the project or the people associated with the project.

Intermittently, when rambling in a chest of drawers, I find the WW II Pacific Theater special, laminated, permanent pass and service medals. Occasionally, I try to connect with a Baker Boy; I place notices in various social media: "WW II Pacific Veteran BB 13 seeks to contact BB 1 through BB 12." I have not received a response.

I continue as I am in life as it is. I continue to believe in and to act in the interest of my country. I continue to believe in and to work for the benefit of government when government believes in and works for the benefit of citizens.

I know from training and experience that America is always just a president away from issuing rain checks in the form of executive orders to citizens who demand due process and other constitutional guarantees. From training and experience, I make choices readily between a president and my country. It is my duty. I am Baker Boy 13, veteran and American citizen.

**A Letter to My Dead Half-sister.**

Dearest Carol:

During your life, I did not acknowledge you as my sister, half or otherwise. When we were children, I blamed you for taking Dad away from me; it was no-fault of yours. I also blamed you for taking Christmas away; it was your birthday.

Mother was too proud to remain married to a man who, during the marriage, impregnated another woman. Mother left taking me with her and got a divorce, freeing Dad to do his duty and marry Eloise, your mother.

It was a lasting union. You, Eloise, and Dad lived together as a family until Dad died.

Throughout our childhood years, I both ignored and trivialized you. I did not refer to or introduced you as "my sister." You always referred to and treated me as your "brother."

*Even when the knife I threw at you struck your leg, you did not tell anyone to protect me from punishment.*

As adults, we spoke briefly; I was always "busy" or "in a hurry." You tried hard to be to me "my sister." You fitted beautifully, physically and spiritually, into your six-foot frame. Your musical gift was extraordinary. When you played your piano rendition of Debussy's *Clair de Lune*, I too was captivated and listened intensely, while intently pretending not to.

54

You were proud of me: "My brother" the "soldier," the "college man," the "lawyer," the "judge;" you, bragging about your brother, beating a distant drum for your brother as your brother paraded proudly through life far from and without you.

Eloise died; you were alone (and perhaps lonely). Often, you asked me to visit you. Once, on a sudden whim when I was in Baltimore attending a conference, I called and arranged to visit you during the conference's lunch interval.

When I arrived at your assisted-living building, you were waiting at the building entrance, and you were ecstatic when you saw me. I asked the taxi driver to return for me in two hours.

After introducing me to half the residents as your brother, you showed me your small living quarters and continually tried to serve me food or drink. You pleaded with me to stay for dinner (I knew that in the dining hall at dinner, you would introduce me as your brother to the residents to whom I had not been introduced). I said, "No." Your face contorted as if slapped by disappointment; whatever hope you had evanesced and dissipated into a vapor of realism; you folded your arms across your chest, and your body wilted into a habituated slump.

As we waited at the building entrance for the taxi to arrive to return me to the conference, you held my hand. I pretended not to notice the plea in your eyes begging me to take you with me, even if only for a little while. Your eyes teared up when you asked me to come back to see you after the conference. As I said goodbye, I said I would try; we both knew I would not. As I taxied out of your life, I looked back and watched you fade into the distance, left behind for the last time.

You died alone and undiscovered for days.

I did not attend your funeral. I attended Dad's funeral; I attended Eloise's funeral. I did not attend your funeral and do not know why.

Carol, I am sorry. I express sorrow that you cannot hear, see, or feel. You are dead. Sorrow is a living thing. This sorrow lives in me and is uniquely mine.

I look into the backyard of my life through the rearview mirror of my memory, see you in the audience, and I feel blessed. Thank you.

Carol, I acknowledge you; I forgive me.

Carol, my sister, goodbye.

Your brother,
Felix.

**Oh, No, Honey!**

We were so, so careful and so, so discrete. We knew that Dr. Wilkerson, my therapist, knew. We were certain that she was the only person at Menninger Clinic who knew about us, you and me – you, the night, supervising, psychiatric nurse with a beauteous, five foot-ten-inch body stowed into a white uniform, a nurse's cap hairpinned to your blond hair, and the mandatory name tag, "Miss Hitner" fastened to your uniform; and I, the law school student and an outpatient, working nights as a psychiatric nurse's aide.

Do you remember the night we found out that everyone knew?

You, and Mrs Anderson (the night supervising nurse's aide, a longtime employee who had "seen it all," average everything – glasses, height, weight, gray hair), and Miss Meister (a nurse's aide, caring, long black hair tightly knotted into a bun, a round face atop a rounded, curvy, short body) were making the hourly rounds on the psychiatric ward. I was staffing the nurses' station as I studied law-class notes.

We were not concerned about the two of you without a male aide doing the rounds on the minimum-security ward. It was after midnight; patients were in bed; and you had a skillful and pleasant relationship with the two patients (Gene Tierney and William Inge) who made the most demands of staff during a night.

Startled by a soft shout, "Mr. Neals! Mr. Neals!" I rushed

to the door of the station and saw Miss Meister standing in the doorway of a patient's room; she beckoned rapidly while saying in a loud whisper, "Hurry. We need help!"

I ran up the hall and into the patient's room. The patient, immobilized in a cold wetpack, had sunk his teeth into your left forearm and, ignoring all pleas, refused to let go.

I began to choke the patient to force him to release his bite. You exclaimed, "Oh, no, Honey!" Following an immobile, silent moment, you gushed, "I mean, Mr. Neals."

Mrs. Anderson and Miss Meister exchanged smiles and glances. Mrs. Anderson retorted, "We know who you mean."

The patient released his bite when he laughed.

Public-knowledge having laughed at our "discreetness," we cautiously accepted the public knowledge of our affair.

When you held me after that, I would ecstatically caress the bite marks and orgastically exclaim, "Oh, yes, Honey! – I mean, Miss Hitner."

**Bus 77.**

Community Line bus 77 (Morristown), traveled a 35-mile trip between Port Authority, New York City, and Morristown, New Jersey.

The blue and white bus 77 was interesting and provoking. Well, not the bus, the ridership. The ridership illustrated the racial divide that existed in suburban New Jersey.

Bus 77 to Morristown left from Port Authority, every hour on the hour, from 6 a.m. until midnight during weekdays, usually carrying a racially integrated ridership through the Lincoln Tunnel into New Jersey, onto NJ Route 3, pass the Meadowlands, and onto Garden State Parkway South. Bus 77 exited the parkway at Exit 147, "Springdale Avenue, East Orange."

The Intersection of Springdale Avenue and Parkway Drive was a major bus stop in East Orange. That was my stop. That was the bus stop for most of the black ridership of bus 77. At that stop, the complexion of the ridership changed. From East Orange to Morristown, the ridership on bus 77 was predominantly white.

I first saw Karen on a Friday evening as I was standing in a line of people waiting in Port Authority to board bus 77 Morristown. A young Black couple got into the waiting line behind me and began to perform a passionate scene expressing the misery and carnality of their "Goodnight" separation.

The bus arrived, and my attention and efforts shifted to getting a seat on the always-overcrowded vehicle. I sat in the first available seat next to a window. The actor from the platform love scene immediately took the seat next to me. She was alone and appeared unaffected by the love scene on the platform. From her appearance, one would think the love scene was imagined.

After the bus left Port Authority, she and I talked. Her name was Karen; she was pretty, twenty-four years old, petite, pecan-brown complexion, short black hair with bangs above big, brown poignant eyes.

Karen shared an apartment in East Orange with her boyfriend (not the actor in the Port Authority love scene). Her parents were divorced. Her father lived in New York. Her mother lived in New Jersey. Neither parent married again. Karen was job hunting and asked if I could help her find a job.

A few days after the bus trip, I telephonically introduced Karen to a client and friend, Peggy Conway, a New York City real estate broker. Karen began to work part-time for Peggy; they became friends.

As soon as her finances allowed, Karen ended the affair with her New Jersey boyfriend and moved from the apartment they shared in New Jersey. She accused him of drug use and physical abuse. While looking for an apartment, Karen stayed with her mother in New Jersey. Karen frequently complained that the relationship with her mother was not amicable, and at any opportunity, Karen would stay with her father in New York.

After her father's death, Karen and I had conversations at various times during trips to New Jersey on bus 77 and during meetings and social gatherings with Peggy and other people. In those conversations, Karen discussed her life, her love affairs, her drug use; and often, in a confessional tone, she referred to "that thing with my father."

Karen's narration never changed. She thought her father to be more understanding and accepting of her behavior than her mother. After a late, late party in Manhattan on a Friday night, New Jersey seemed a long way away; she was dizzy and in no mood to hear a lecture from her mother. Karen decided to stay the night at her father's apartment in Manhattan.

When she arrived at her father's apartment, her head throbbed, and she was nauseated. She explained to her father why she did not want to go Jersey and asked if she could stay the night. He okayed her overnight stay; he was aware of and worried about both her lifestyle and her relationship with her mother.

Karen did not keep clothes at her father's. When she stayed overnight in New York, she wore a pajama top or a large tee shirt of his as a nightshirt. In the one-bedroom apartment, she slept on a pullout sofa in the living room.

When she awoke Saturday morning, her nausea had passed, but she was still dizzy, had a severe stiff neck, and a persistent headache. She went into her father's bedroom to ask if he had any medications. Being dizzy, she sat on the side of his bed. Her father began to massage her neck and shoulders. Karen felt some relief from the pain and, unthinkingly (she said), lowered the nightshirt from her shoulders and stretched out face down on the bed to allow him to continue the massage. Neither commented and remained silent during the entire event.

She did not remember when the touch became intimate or when they started to have sex. She remembered that they both had an intense orgasm. Afterward, they both felt guilty and silently and awkwardly tiptoed around each other until Karen left the apartment. They never talked to each other about the experience.

Three weeks after the episode, Karen called her father, told him that she was pregnant, and asked him for financial help. They met; he gave her money for an abortion and pleaded with her not to tell her mother about the pregnancy. Karen arranged to have an abortion, accepted several sums of money from her father and kept him informed of her actions before and after the abortion, including information that she had been carrying a boy child. She never said to her father that he fathered her pregnancy.

Within a month after Karen's abortion, her father had a massive heart attack and died. He died without knowing that Karen was (and knew that she was) pregnant when she arrived at his apartment that Friday night. He died not knowing that he had not impregnated Karen.

After her father's death, Karen's life spun between drugs and affairs. Peggy died. Karen and I chose different social paths and lost all contact with each other.

Years passed. In a chance encounter in Tribeca, Manhattan, I met and talked with a friend of Karen's, Christine. Christine told me about Karen. Karen completed treatment at a New York City drug rehabilitation center. At the center, she met her fiancé, whom she was to marry in a few weeks at New York City Hall.

Delighted by the news from Christine, I offered to give and host a wedding party for Karen at Valentina's Restaurant on Reade Street in Manhattan, four blocks from City Hall where the marriage was scheduled to take place. I never spoke to or saw Karen; through Christine, I coordinated the party with the planned wedding date.

At Valentina's on the scheduled day and time, I hosted a table prepared for the bride and groom and wedding guests. I waited at the private table with empty chairs, food, champagne, and flowers. No one appeared.

I invited strangers to the party. As guests at a wedding party should, we ate the food and drank the champagne. Among conversations about the unseen, unspoken, recollections, and questions, we toasted Karen and husband a future of happiness and good fortune.

In a celebrant mood, we left the withered flowers, empty bottles, food scraps, used paper, and soiled plastic to be bundled and discarded with other unrecyclable and recyclable waste.

**Conversations with Mr. Dillard.**

Mr. Dillard is a next-door neighbor of my son, Julien. Sight of Mr. Dillard and Julien together remind me of a gathering of weight lifters and body builders. Both did both. Each has an easily recognized physique of an athlete. Of the two, Mr. Dillard is a smidgen taller (about 6' 3"), 10 to 15 pounds heavier (weighing maybe 215 pounds), with carefully cut hair and trimmed beard, both graying.

During visits to Julien's yard-barbeques and holiday celebrations, Mr. Dillard and I talk briefly. We always stand when talking to each other. Mr. Dillard looks slightly up at me (taller [6'5"] and thinner [150 pounds]); our matching physical asymmetries (mine that of a half-finished scarecrow) pose in a conspiratorial posture.

We imperil ideas, concepts, beliefs, and the perils of knowledge in our talks. Mr. Dillard makes the same request at the end of every conversation. His fifty-something, year-old eyes stare directly into my eighty-eight-year-old eyes, he smiles and says,

"I want the book. Just leave me the book."

My smile is my reply as we part.

We both know. I know he knows I know he knows as we talk, he is writing the book.

We both know. I know he knows I know he knows as we talk, I am writing the book.

We both know. I know he knows I know he knows as we talk, we are writing the book.

We both know we both know life writes the book.

We both know we both know there is one book.

We both know we both know, Mr. Dillard and I.

**Vision.**


You say,
"What a beautiful day!"
And, "I love the rain!"
Your words blossom
from your lips.

I struggle to understand.
Questions explode in my mind.
My heart beats chaotically.

How? How
do you see beauty in a day?
Feel love in rain?

Are they learned or acquired
perceptions?

Or at birth,
did life gift-wrap you
in rapture?

Conception abducted me
from everything
and budded me,
life inside life.

Birth aborted me,
life out of life
into livelihood
without perception
of personhood.

**Understood by Misunderstanding.**
*(Understood by Misunderstanding.)*

I understand
*(we understand),*

why I was not understood
*(why we were not understood).*

I was not understood
*(we were not understood).*

by misunderstanding
*(by misunderstanding)*

"mental retardation" and "schizophrenia"
*("mental retardation" and "schizophrenia").*

I understand
*(we understand),*

why I was misunderstood
*(why we were misunderstood);*

I was misunderstood
*(we were misunderstood)*

by understanding
*by understanding*

"mental retardation" and "schizophrenia"
*("mental retardation" and "schizophrenia").*

I understand

*(we understand)*
I am understood
*(we are understood)*

by understanding
*(by understanding)*

misunderstanding
*(misunderstanding)*

of "autism"
*(of "autism").*

**Recursion.**

thought
= exact exactly
= exactly in exactly
= exactly out exactly
= exact exactly
= thought.
thought = thought.

effect
= exact exactly
= exactly in exactly
= exactly out exactly
= exact exactly
= effect.
effect = effect.

thought = thought.
effect = effect.
(thought = thought) = (effect = effect).
thought = effect.

thought = 1.
effect = 1.
(thought = 1) = (effect = 1).
$(1 = 1) = (1 = 1) = (1 = 1)$.
$(1 = 1) = 1$.
$1 = \infty$.

**Disambiguation.**


What I did when I did
what I did is what I do
when I do what I do.

When I did what I did
when I did what I did
is when I do what I do
when I do what I do.

Where I did what I did
when I did what I did
is where I do what I do
when I do what I do.

How I did what I did
when I did what I did
is how I do what I do
when I do what I do.

Why I did what I did
when I did what I did
is why I do what I do
when I do what I do.

What, when, where,
how, and why
I do what I did
are why, how, where,
when, and what
I am and who.

**Golden Acts.**


Could and should
and did, did
what could've
and should've.

Could and should
but didn't, didn't
what could've.
and should've.

Couldn't and shouldn't
and did, did
what shouldn't've.

Couldn't and shouldn't
and didn't, didn't
what couldn't
and shouldn't.

Could and shouldn't
and did, did
what could
and shouldn't've.

Could and shouldn't
and didn't, didn't
what could've
and shouldn't.

Couldn't and should
and did, did

what should've.

Could, couldn't,
could've, couldn't've,
should, shouldn't,
should've, shouldn't've,
did and didn't
are golden acts.

Made in the USA
Middletown, DE
15 September 2017